Finances
for Today's Catholic
FAMILY

FINANCIAL FOUNDATIONS FOR THE FAMILY is a nonprofit organization dedicated to sharing God's principles on finances found in Sacred Scripture and the Teaching and Tradition of the Catholic Church.

If you would like more information on Financial Foundations for the Family, contact us at our office listed below.

FINANCIAL FOUNDATIONS FOR THE FAMILY
P.O. Box 890998
Temecula, California 92589-0998
USA

Phone 909-699-7066
Fax 909-308-4539

Finances
for Today's
Catholic
FAMILY

by Philip Lenahan

Illustrations by Terry Sexton

FINANCIAL FOUNDATIONS
FOR THE FAMILY

Scripture texts used in this work are taken from the New American Bible. The Old Testament of the New American Bible © 1970 by the Confraternity of Christian Doctrine (CCD), Washington, D.C. (Books 1 Samuel to 2 Macaccabees © 1969); Revised New Testament of the New American Bible Copyright © 1986 CCD; Revised Psalms of the New American Bible Copyright © 1991 CCD.

ISBN 0-9652869-0-8

Printed in the United States of America

Table of Contents

Introduction

Families are under tremendous pressure today, and finances often add to this pressure because they are a major source of anxiety and worry. Families report common issues: learning to live within their means; deciding if both spouses will work outside the home; abusing credit cards with consequent buildup of debt; and inability to save for future needs.

Given that the divorce rate in the United States is about 50 percent and that most couples who divorce say that financial issues were a primary cause, there is clearly need for sound instruction on how a family should handle money. If you are widowed or a divorced head of household, of course, careful management is even more critical. But whether you are single, preparing for marriage, or celebrating your twenty-fifth anniversary, the good news is that finances need not remain a mystery or cause of frustration.

The purpose of this guide is twofold. First, by drawing on the wisdom found in Sacred Scripture and the Teaching and Tradition of the Catholic Church, it will help you develop a Christian attitude toward your family finances. Second, it will provide basic and very practical financial planning tools in a step-by-step format so that you can *take control* of your finances.

The guide draws on our counseling experience and uses the same tools we have developed in that counseling. Our objective is to keep family budgeting as simple and streamlined as possible.

It is my hope that as you seek God's will and apply His wisdom in your daily lives, His peace will reign in your hearts. God bless you!

In Christ,

Philip Lenahan

Philip Lenahan
President

Part 1:Attitude

Why talk about money?

The Survey Says:

Take a look at these startling statistics about the state of family finances in America:

- 49% don't pay their bills on time.*

- 65% don't do a good job of staying out of debt.*

- 65% don't balance their checkbook.*

- 82% don't adequately save for future needs.*

- Charitable giving averages less than 2% for all Americans and about 1% for American Catholics.

- 50% of all marriages end in divorce.

- A majority of those getting divorces point to finances as one of the primary causes of the breakup.

I'm not sure I would have believed these statistics had it not been for the number of families I have counseled who struggle day in and day out with their finances.

Take the Smiths (not their real name). They had never received instruction on the basics of managing their money. All they knew was that *every month* there was a little more month left at the end of the money.

When they saw the credit card offers in the mail, they thought they had been given a solution to their chronic shortfall. They never planned to become so dependent upon the credit cards, but it just happened. Before they knew it, they had run up debts of $20,000 — in addition

---

* *David Michaelson and Associates for Mastercard International.*

1

to their mortgage and car loan. With an annual income of about $40,000, they felt overwhelmed and helpless. The father described this burden as a lead weight and chain attached to his leg.

Unfortunately, based on the phone calls and letters I receive, this scenario is all too common in our society.

The most alarming statistic, and maybe the most surprising, is that a majority of people obtaining a divorce state that *one of the primary causes* of the breakup involves money issues. When the statistics showing how poorly we manage our money are combined with that statistic, we can see how explosive money problems are, and how much human damage they can do.

If we're going to have strong families, we must get a handle on our finances. More important, we need to develop and foster an attitude about money that is in line with the will of God. That's what this guide and it's companion materials are all about. When we combine the ageless principles found in the Teaching and Tradition of the Holy Catholic Church with practical and easy-to-understand financial planning tools, we are released from the chain and lead weight of money worries and we are set financially free.

The Problem

The first step in solving a problem is to understand what the problem is. I propose that our money problems are so substantial because we have allowed a wall to separate our faith from our finances.

Faith   Finances

When that happens, the wisdom found in Sacred Scripture and Church Teaching gets pushed aside and the consumer mentality of our society takes over. Our insatiable appetite for more things is fed by the easy availability of credit — and all of a sudden you've got a financial disaster on your hands.

Recall the scene in the Old Testament where Joshua, in his old age, reminds the Israelites of their covenant with the Lord and poses this question: "If it does not please you to serve the Lord, decide today whom you will serve, the gods your fathers served beyond the river or the gods of the Amorites in whose country you are dwelling. *As for me and my household, we will serve the Lord*" (Joshua 24:15).

Fast forward to the Sermon on the Mount where our Lord provides His disciples with the foundations for living a truly Christian life. He says, "Remember, where your treasure is, there your heart is also. . . No man can serve two masters. He will either hate one and love the other or be attentive to one and despise the other. You cannot give yourself to God and money. . . Your heavenly Father knows all that you need. Seek first his kingship over you, his way of holiness, and all these things will be given you besides." (Mt. 6:21–33).

Materialism   Kingdom of God

Scripture and Church teaching set forth two clear, but divergent paths that we can take with our finances. The materialistic way of the world is characterized by love of self and love of things, while God's way is characterized by love of God and love of neighbor. The world's way leads to bondage, anxiety, and worry, while God's way leads to freedom, peace, and contentment.

How can you tell if you are following the way of the world with your finances? Recall the statistics at the beginning of this chapter and consider the following scenarios:

- Is there always more month left at the end of the paycheck?

- Do you find that your charitable giving is done after all of your other bills are paid rather than from your first fruits — and as a result, it falls far short of the Scriptural tithe, or one-tenth?

- Do you pay your entire credit card balance off every month — or is consumer debt accumulating?

- Do you have a planned savings program where money is set aside every month for future needs, or are you spending all of your current income?

The Solution — The *Right* Attitude

For too long, we have let that wall separate our faith life from how we handle our money. It's time we break it down. We must recognize that how we manage our finances is an outside indicator of our interior life.

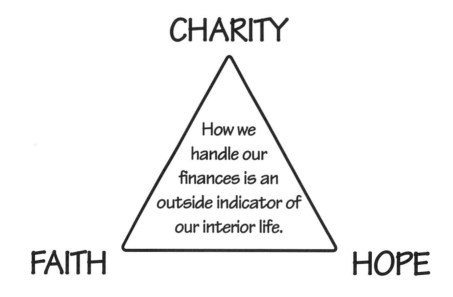

CHARITY

How we handle our finances is an outside indicator of our interior life.

FAITH   HOPE

What *should* our attitude about money be? How can we develop that attitude and be confident that it is in God's will?

As always, when we search for guidance on how to live a life pleasing to God, Sacred Scripture and the Church's Teaching and Tradition offer a rich source of instruction. This holds true for our attitude toward money as well. There are several hundred direct references to money in the Bible — and Jesus dedicated about *two-thirds* of His parables to the proper handling of money. The new *Catechism of the Catholic Church* offers a wealth of information to help us develop the proper attitude toward material things. Sacred Scripture and the Teaching and Tradition of the Church provide a road map for leading a life of holiness and virtue. Through studying and meditating on them, we will be able to put money in its proper place.

We can summarize the teaching on money found in Sacred Scripture and the Teaching and Tradition of the Catholic Church with the following diagram:

"A Life of Virtue"

Common Good

Mercy   Charity

Compassion   Benevolence

Providence   Almsgiving

Sacred Scripture

Teaching & Tradition of the Church

Temperance   Responsibility

Self-mastery   Generosity

Justice   Sacrifice

Love of Neighbor

Consumer Mentality · · · · · · · · · Virtue

Picture an old-fashioned scale. On one side lies the consumer mentality, and on the other rests the practice of virtue. In our society, the consumer mentality far outweighs virtue, and, as a result, our lives are out of balance. Sacred Scripture and Church Teaching provide the much-needed counterweights to restore equilibrium.

When we apply the virtues to the management of our finances, we can be confident we are following God's will in this important area of our lives. Because of this, no matter what circumstances we find ourselves in, we will be full of His peace and contentment.

I have summarized these virtues into *five key principles* that a family can use to guide their financial decision making. These principles provide a balanced approach to managing your money in accord with God's plan and when combined with the practical tools provided in Part II, they allow you to *take control* of your family finances.

Five Principles You Can Bank On

1. Seek First the Kingdom of God.

2. Trust in the Providence of God.

3. Develop a Charitable Spirit.

4. Practice the Virtue of Temperance.

5. Develop Personal Responsibility.

Five Principles You Can Bank On

Let's go through a brief discussion of these principles. At the end of each section, you will find a self/group-study utilizing references from Sacred Scripture and the *Catechism of the Catholic Church*. These readings and questions will help you develop the *right* attitude toward material things. If you are a couple, I recommend that you complete the self/group-study together.

Principle #1 — Seek First the Kingdom of God.

Allow me to quote once again from our Lord's Sermon on the Mount, where he says, "Do not lay up for yourselves an earthly treasure. Moths and rust corrode; thieves break in and steal. Make it your practice instead to store up heavenly treasure, which neither moths nor rust corrode nor thieves break in and steal. Remember, where your treasure is, there your heart is also. . . No man can serve two masters. He will either hate one and love the other or be attentive to one and despise the other. You cannot give yourself to God and money" (Mt. 6:19–21).

We must take care to understand what our Lord is saying and what the Church teaches regarding material things. Money and other "things" are part of God's creation and are good. The problem arises when we allow these things to become an end in themselves rather than a means of furthering the Gospel message. Our society has become a society of "having" as opposed to one of "being." A "having" society encourages an attitude of "what's in it for me" that disregards the call to Gospel charity and instead focuses on self. This is what our Lord is warning us about in these verses.

After the fall of communism in Eastern Europe, many bishops and the Holy Father expressed great concern for the faith of these people who had remained incredibly strong through terrible years of persecution. Why were Church leaders concerned now that the people were *free?* During the years of persecution, they faced an enemy they could see. Now, the Holy Father and the region's bishops saw a new enemy, a much more subtle enemy, which they knew had done so much damage to the faith in the Western world. That enemy is the prevalent consumer attitude, which transforms a society from one of "being" to one of "having."

The way we can fight that enemy is to love the Lord with all our heart, soul and mind (Mt. 22:37–38). But how do we keep God first in our lives amidst all of our daily responsibilities and "to do" lists? Time and commitment are key ingredients to any successful relationship and our relationship with the Lord is no different. Here are some practical suggestions to help you "Seek First the Kingdom of God."

- Dedicate each day to our Lord upon rising with a morning offering.

- Read Sacred Scripture or the writings of the Saints for 10 or 15 minutes each day.

- Attend Mass daily if possible. If not Mass, perhaps a brief visit to our Lord in the Blessed Sacrament.

- Pray the Angelus at midday.

- Pray a mystery of the Rosary in honor of the Blessed Virgin each day.

- Complete a five-minute review of your day upon going to bed.

- Make a weekly holy hour (Eucharistic adoration).

- Receive the Sacrament of Reconciliation every two weeks.

It is through the sacramental life that we are able to deepen our relationship with our Lord.

Self/Group-Study

Read the following passages from Scripture: Jeremiah 9:22–23; Matthew 6:19–33; Matthew 22:37–38; Mark 8:34–35; Luke 12:16–20; 1 Timothy 6:10.

Read the following sections of the *Catechism of the Catholic Church*: 1; 27; 222–227; 543–546; 1210; 1391–1398; 1468; 1723–1724; 1814–1816; 1942; 2083–2084; 2095–2100; 2558–2559.

Answer the following questions:
What do the Scriptures and *Catechism* say is the reason for our existence?

_____

_____

_____

_____

_____

_____

_____

_____

_____

_____

_____

_____

_____

_____

_____

_____

_____

_____

_____

_____

What concern does Scripture express about money?

_____

_____

_____

_____

_____

_____

_____

_____

_____

_____

_____

_____

_____

The *Catechism* speaks of the implications of faith in God. Describe these.

_____

_____

_____

_____

_____

_____

_____

_____

_____

_____

_____

_____

_____

_____

_____

Describe how prayer and participation in the Sacraments help us "Seek First the Kingdom of God."

_____

_____

_____

_____

_____

_____

_____

_____

_____

_____

_____

_____

_____

_____

_____

Principle #2 — Trust in the Providence of God.

Let's return to the Sermon on the Mount. Our Lord continues, saying, "Stop worrying, then, over questions like, 'what are we to eat, or what are we to drink, or what are we to wear?' The unbelievers are always running after these things. Your heavenly Father knows all that you need. Seek first his kingship over you, his way of holiness and all these things will be given you besides" (Mt. 6:31–33).

The key word in this passage is "heavenly Father." We have a Father in heaven who loves us so much that He gave His only Son for our redemption (Jn. 3:16). His desire is for us to trust completely in Him as beloved children.

Our society has made incredible advances in science and technology over the last several decades, and these are good when used in ways consistent with God's plan. However, one drawback is we can begin to believe that we are in control of everything, and, as a result, forget to trust in God. The *Pastoral Constitution on the Church in the Modern World* of the Second Vatican Council states it this way: "Today, particularly by means of science and technology, [man] has extended his mastery over almost the whole of nature, and still continues to extend it. . . . As a result, *where formerly man looked especially to supernatural forces for blessings, he now secures many of these benefits himself, thanks to his own efforts.*"

It's easy to see how this issue of control can influence our attitude toward family finances. We begin to believe that we are in complete control and are not dependent upon God for our daily sustenance. We can also forget to give thanks *daily* for His provision.

One of the great accounts of Divine Providence in the Old Testament is the story of Elijah and the widow (1 Kings 17:7–16). "After some time, however, the brook ran dry, because no rain had fallen in the land. So the Lord said to him: 'Move on to Zarephath of Sidon and stay there. I have designated a widow there to provide for you.' He left and went to Zarephath. As he arrived at the entrance of the city, a widow was gathering sticks there; he called out to her, 'Please bring me a small cupful of water to drink.' She left to get it, and he called out after her, 'Please bring along a bit of bread.' 'As the Lord, your God, lives,' she answered, 'I have nothing baked; *there is only a handful of flour in my jar and a little oil in my jug.* Just now I was collecting a couple of sticks to go in and prepare something for myself and my son; *when we have eaten it, we shall die.'* 'Do not be afraid,' Elijah said to her. 'Go and do as you propose. But first make me a little cake and bring it to me. Then you can prepare something for yourself and your son. *For the Lord, the God of Israel, says, "The jar of flour shall not go empty, nor the jug of oil run dry, until the day when the Lord sends rain upon the earth."'* She left and did as Elijah had said. She was able to eat for a year, and he and her son as well; the jar of flour did not go empty, nor the jug of oil run dry, as the Lord had foretold through Elijah."*

What heroic faith this widow had. We are called to this same faith, knowing that our heavenly Father will provide.

12

Self/Group-Study

Read the following passages from Scripture: Proverbs 16:3; Proverbs 16:9; Proverbs 30:7–9; Matthew 6:24–33; 1 Timothy 6:17–19.

   Read the following sections of the *Catechism of the Catholic Church*: 144–149; 219; 302–314; 322; 1817–1821; 2828–2837.

Answer the following questions:
The verses from Proverbs describe our willingness to submit ourselves to the will of God. This calls for obedience. Summarize what the *Catechism* says about obedience.

_____

_____

_____

_____

_____

_____

_____

_____

_____

_____

_____

_____

_____

_____

_____

_____

_____

_____

_____

_____

_____

_____

_____

God's love for us is compared to the love of a father for his children. In Matthew, Jesus reminds us of this love and tells us not to worry over our daily needs. He wants us to seek Him first and promises that our needs will be met. Are you preoccupied with the things and worries of this world? What steps can you take to eliminate these unnecessary worries?

_____

_____

_____

_____

_____

_____

_____

_____

_____

_____

_____

Some people may take trusting in God's providence to mean they have no responsibility. Timothy tells us to be rich in good works and the *Catechism* speaks clearly of how God desires to work through us. St. Ignatius Loyola said, "Pray as if everything depended on God, and work as if everything depended on you." Summarize the balance the Lord is asking for between trust in Him and personal responsibility.

_____

_____

_____

_____

_____

_____

_____

_____

_____

_____

_____

Principle #3 — Develop a Charitable Spirit.

Our Lord calls us to love our neighbors as ourselves and this principle encompasses all of the works of mercy which the Catholic Church has tirelessly promoted since being founded by Christ. Even though this principle is broad in application, I want to focus here on the act of tithing.

Tithing is one of the most misunderstood concepts in Christian living today. Many sermons focus on funding new buildings, school programs, or missionary activities, all of which are worthy endeavors. But when we limit our understanding of tithing to providing for the physical needs of the Church, we have missed its *primary* purpose as outlined in Sacred Scripture and Church Teaching. *Tithing was given to us by God as a way of strengthening our relationship with Him.*

In the prophetic book of Malachi, we are told, "Since the days of your fathers you have turned aside from my statutes, and have not kept them. Return to me, and I will return to you, says the Lord of hosts. Yet you say, 'How must we return?' Dare a man rob God? Yet you are robbing me! And you say, 'How do we rob you?' In tithes and in offerings! You are indeed accursed, for you, the whole nation, rob me. Bring the whole tithe into the storehouse, That there may be food in my house, and try me in this, says the Lord of hosts: Shall I not open for you the floodgates of heaven, to pour down blessing upon you without measure?" (Mal. 3:7–10).

These words of wisdom apply to us today as much as they did to the Israelites of the Old Testament (Malachi 3:6). We become so distracted by the daily activities of our lives and our desire to succeed that we forget our Lord. Tithing provides the way to rearrange our priorities and turn our hearts back to our loving Father. It is the tool we *need* to overcome the materialistic attitude so prevalent in our society.

We have seen case after case of people who have sought happiness through the pursuit of material goods, only to realize that these never lead to fulfillment. Instead, the pressure of maintaining a lifestyle beyond one's means, especially if it is built on a mountain of credit, often leads to a breakup of the family and a loss of faith.

People who tithe, on the other hand, find that the worries and anxieties they once had are replaced by contentment as they learn to place love of God and neighbor above their desire for things. They also find that they become much better stewards of the resources God has given them. When families with financial problems such as habitual overspending, high debt levels and a lack of savings apply God's principles for handling money, they begin to bring order to what has been a chaotic situation.

You can use the following guidelines to implement tithing as part of your family finances:

Remember that . .

- All we have comes from God. He owns it all (Deut. 10:14).

- With rare exceptions, we should view the tithe as an obligation to God. It is the minimum called for in Sacred Scripture (Malachi 3:8–10).

- Our tithe is to be a response from the heart. Jesus condemns the pharisees for becoming legalistic in their religious practices. He tells them to continue their good works but to change their motive to one of love of God and neighbor (Luke 11:39–42). The Sermon on the Mount should guide our charitable spirit (Mt. 5:3–12).

- We are called to tithe from our first fruits (Exodus 23:19). By paying God first, we develop a habit of generosity that orders our activities toward the Kingdom of Heaven (*Catechism of the Catholic Church* 1818).

- Through tithing we learn to place our trust in God's providence. He has promised to provide for our needs (Mt. 6:30–34).

- Almsgiving is provided by God as one form of penance along with prayer and fasting (Tobit 12:8–10; *Catechism* 1434).

- The Lord promises blessings for this step of obedience. These may be in the form of a closer relationship with Him, an improved family life, or material blessings. If we are blessed with an abundance of wealth, it is important to recall Paul's words in 2 Corinthians 9:8–10, where he says, "God can multiply His favors among you so that you may always have enough of everything *and even a surplus for good works."*

- God can multiply our resources and make 90 percent go further than 100 percent. Read the stories of the widows and the miracle of the multiplication of the loaves and fish (1 Kings 17:7–16; 2 Kings 4:1–7; Mt. 14:13–21).

- We are called to be cheerful givers (Acts 20:35; 2 Corinthians 9:6-7). A typical response from persons who tithe is that they enjoy paying their tithing "bills" as compared to their regular bills.

- Our giving should be planned, not done haphazardly (1 Corinthians 16:1–2).

The scriptural principle is to tithe on your increase, so you can use 10 percent of your after-tax income, but over time, don't be surprised if your heart is moved to share even more. In the usual situation, we suggest you give half of your tithe to your parish and the remainder to other worthy organizations. Remember to review your amount periodically and adjust for changes in income. Finally, ask yourself the following question: would God be satisfied with your charitable works if He saw your checkbook?

The table below shows amounts based on varying incomes and rates of giving. You can use it to compute your tithe.

Income Level	1%*	10%**
100,000	1,000	10,000
90,000	900	9,000
80,000	800	8,000
70,000	700	7,000
60,000	600	6,000
50,000	500	5,000
40,000	400	4,000
30,000	300	3,000
20,000	200	2,000
10,000	100	1,000

*The average American Catholic gives about 1%.
**God's minimum as outlined in Sacred Scripture is 10%

I'd like to share a story that captures the focus of these first three principles. I vividly remember the first counseling session I had with one couple. After we had discussed the concept of tithing, the husband seemed pretty well convinced based on the Scripture references I had provided. But the wife was angry with me, and believe me, I could understand why. They were not well off financially, and she commented on how her children's shoes had holes in them. Here I was adding what appeared to her as an additional burden. The pain in her face was evident as we discussed this. We finished the session and set a time for our second meeting a month later. Imagine my surprise when her attitude toward tithing had completely turned around. After she and her husband had left that first meeting, he had asked that they try tithing for a few months. While still uncomfortable, she went along with her husband's request and they found that they made it through the month and experienced a joy at placing this area in God's hands.

Later I received a Christmas card from the couple with the following note, "Through your counseling, we learned that all things are possible with prayer and our rich Catholic faith. Because you reached out to us, we are in our first home for Christmas, can pay cash for our gifts, and still keep afloat. Thank you so very much. You gave us the tools we'll use over the course of our lifetime and a legacy we can pass on to our sons."

It's important you know I'm not teaching a prosperity message. This family had to make some sacrifices to bring things in line. But listen to the joy in that message! We are called to be obedient in the area of tithing. I encourage you to try it for six months as Malachi tells us and see what blessings our Lord has in store for you.

Self/Group-Study

Read the following passages from Scripture: Deuteronomy 10:14; Tobit 4:5–11; Proverbs 3:27–28; Sirach 35:1–11; Malachi 3:8–10; Matthew 6:1–4; Matthew 25:33–46; Mark 12:41–44; Luke 10:25–37; 2 Corinthians 9:6–13; James 2:14–17.

Read the following sections of the *Catechism of the Catholic Church:* 575; 1032; 1434; 1438; 1813; 1818; 1822–29; 1832; 1844; 1849; 1855; 1889; 1969; 2055; 2094; 2101; 2439–40; 2443–49; 2462–63; 2544–47.

Answer the following questions:
Malachi and Sirach tell us that God will bless those who faithfully tithe. Describe in your own words the relationship between the virtue of hope (especially as relates to trusting in the providence of God), and the virtue of charity.

_____

_____

_____

_____

_____

_____

_____

_____

_____

_____

Some people would say that tithing was only asked for in the Old Testament. After reading these verses, how would you respond to that?

_____

_____

_____

_____

_____

_____

_____

_____

_____

_____

● After having read the Scripture verses and especially the *Catechism* reference 2544–2547, describe "poverty of heart" in your own words.

_____

_____

_____

_____

_____

_____

_____

_____

_____

_____

_____

_____

_____

_____

● Scripture is full of references to the tithe coming from the first fruits (Exodus 23:19; Deut. 18:3–5;26:1–11; Ezek. 44:30 to name a few). What does this mean — and how can you apply the principle in your own life?

_____

_____

_____

_____

_____

_____

_____

_____

_____

_____

_____

_____

_____

●_____

Principle #4 — Practice the Virtue of Temperance.

In 1 Timothy 6:6–11, we read, "There is, of course, great gain in religion — provided one is content with a sufficiency. We brought nothing into this world, nor have we the power to take anything out. If we have food and clothing we have all that we need. Those who want to be rich are falling into temptation and a trap. They are letting themselves be captured by foolish and harmful desires which drag men down to ruin and destruction. The love of money is the root of all evil. Some men in their passion for it have strayed from the faith, and have come to grief amid great pain. Man of God that you are, flee from all this. Instead, seek after integrity, piety, faith, love, steadfastness, and a gentle spirit."

The consumer attitude in our society adds a challenge for families in determining what a "sufficiency" is. When I first sit down to counsel a family, I ask them to describe their current situation. Inevitably, the answer comes back that "there isn't enough money!" This holds true no matter what the income level is. If I were to share a story of how a family of six earning $30,000 per year was living paycheck to paycheck, you could probably relate to their struggle, recognizing that it's not easy to make it today on that amount of money. Would you believe me if I said the same thing about a family earning $90,000 per year? I can hear it now. "*What?* I wish I made that much. We'd have no problem living on that income!"

What's my point here? It's that your family's financial condition isn't as dependent on how much you make so much as on your willingness to live within your means. You may *feel* that all you need is another $10,000 to get out from under your problems, but until you make a conscious decision to live within your means, you will find your appetite for things outstripping your ability to pay for them. The *Catechism of the Catholic Church* captures this attitude well when it states, " Our thirst for another's goods is immense, infinite, never quenched" (2536). I've heard it said another way as well: "Most people don't thank God when their cup runneth over. Instead, they ask for a bigger cup."

When the consumer attitude is combined with an economy based on debt, it becomes all too easy for families to run into trouble. It's not uncommon to receive daily offers in the mail for new credit cards or home equity loans. I recently noticed a billboard for a nationwide bank which took the credit message to a new level as it said, "Take a loan out with your groceries: anytime, anywhere banking." When tempted with these offers, we would do well to remember Proverbs 22:7 where it says "The borrower is the slave of the lender." One could rephrase the bank's offer to say, "Take a loan out with your groceries. Anytime, anywhere *bondage!*"

Temperance is a *key* virtue for today's families. When we are able to moderate our desire for things, we can better avoid the bondage of excessive debt and enjoy the peace and contentment that Paul describes.

Self/Group-Study

Read the following passages from Scripture: Psalm 119:72; Proverbs 8:17–21; Proverbs 21:17; Proverbs 30:7–9; Ecclesiastes 2:10–11; Matthew 5:3; Matthew 6:19–33; Matthew 20:1–16; Mark 8:34–38; Luke 12:16–20; Philippians 4:10–13; Colossians 3:2; 1 Thessalonians 5:16–18; 1 Timothy 6:6–10; 1 John 2:15–17; Philippians 2:3–5; Hebrews 13:5–6.

Read the following sections of the *Catechism of the Catholic Church*: 736; 1434; 1438; 1805; 1809; 1832; 1866; 2043; 2100; 2342; 2409.

Answer the following questions:
Based on the readings, provide a definition of materialism.

_____

_____

_____

_____

_____

_____

_____

_____

_____

_____

_____

The *Catechism* describes self-mastery as a long and exacting work. Applying the recommended readings, describe contentment and the ability to moderate the desire for material things (self-mastery) as it relates in your own life.

_____

_____

_____

_____

_____

_____

_____

_____

_____

Principle #5 — Develop Personal Responsibility.

In Matthew 25:14–30, we read the story of the three servants who were each given silver pieces to invest. Two of the servants were good stewards and diligently managed the money so that the master had a good return on his investment, while the third buried the money. The master rewarded the first two and angrily chastised the third for not managing his affairs well.

The third steward reminds me of those who improperly interpret trusting in the providence of God to mean they have no responsibility. Our Lord couldn't be more clear in this parable that he expects us to use the talents he has given us diligently to further His Kingdom. We are to use our talents to the best of our ability, and to rely on God to fill in where we lack.

The principle of personal responsibility is extremely broad. It encompasses a life of integrity, devotion to your family and excellence in your work. In a word it means good *stewardship* and our Lord wants nothing less!

Self/Group-Study

Read the following sections of the *Catechism of the Catholic Church*: 1803–32; 1835–44; 1914; 2095–96; 2407; 2221–2231; 2427–2429

Using the *Catechism* references cited and the Scripture references noted in each question, answer the following:

How does your dictionary define a steward? Read Matthew 25:14–30, where Jesus tells a parable about stewardship. What is the main point he is making?

_____

_____

_____

_____

_____

_____

_____

_____

_____

_____

_____

_____

_____

● Proverbs 22:7 provides a clear picture of how God views debt. In addition, the issue of cosigning is discussed in Proverbs 6:1–5; 11:15; 17:18; 20:16; and 22:26–27. After reading these verses, summarize in your own words what Scripture tells us about debt and cosigning.

_____

_____

_____

_____

_____

_____

_____

_____

_____

_____

_____

_____

● The following Scripture verses discuss planning, living within your means, saving, investing and inheritance: Proverbs 6:6–11; 20:21; 21:5; 21:20; 27:23; 28:20 and Luke 14:28–30. Read these verses, then summarize in your own words what Scripture tells us about these topics.

_____

_____

_____

_____

_____

_____

_____

_____

_____

_____

● _____

The following Scripture verses contrast excellence in work with laziness: Proverbs 12:27; 13:4; 19:15; 20:4; 21:25; 22:29; 24:30–34 and Colossians 3:17. After reading them, summarize in your own words what Scripture tells us about these issues.

_____

_____

_____

_____

_____

_____

_____

_____

_____

_____

_____

_____

In our society, honesty and integrity are often rare virtues. Read the following passages from Scripture to review what the Lord has to say about these topics: Proverbs 11:1; Luke 16:10–12, and Ephesians 4:28. Summarize in your own words what Scripture tells us about these virtues.

_____

_____

_____

_____

_____

_____

_____

_____

_____

_____

_____

_____

● Today, children are often viewed as a burden rather than a blessing. Read Psalm 127:3–5, Proverbs 1:8, Proverbs 22:6, Matthew 19:14 and Ephesians 6:4 to review what the Lord has to say about children. Compare and contrast this view with what you see in society.

_____

_____

_____

_____

_____

_____

_____

_____

_____

_____

_____

● God calls us to lead a virtuous life. Sacred Scripture and the *Catechism* offer a road map to show us how to live a life pleasing to God. Read Titus 2:1–6; then describe a virtuous life.

_____

_____

_____

_____

_____

_____

_____

_____

_____

_____

_____

_____

●

Summary

These five principles will provide a balance to your family's finances that is sorely lacking in most of our society today. Now it's up to you to make a choice. You can have the weight and chain that comes with the world's ways, or the peace and contentment that comes by submitting your finances to Christ's will.

The late Archbishop Fulton Sheen once related a story in which he described a mint where the coins of a country were produced. In that mint were two molds, a mold of Caesar and a mold of Christ. If we are the coins, we need to ask ourselves a key question. Are we imprinted with Caesar (do we belong to the world), or are we imprinted with Christ (do we belong to God)? It is my hope and prayer that we are all imprinted with Christ!

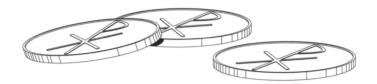

Part II: Building Blocks for Family Finances

Introduction

Now that we have covered the principles found in Sacred Scripture and the Teaching of the Holy Catholic Church, we need to build a bridge that will help you apply those principles to your family finances. This is where the rubber meets the road. Here are the basic financial planning tools that will help you "live your faith through your family finances."

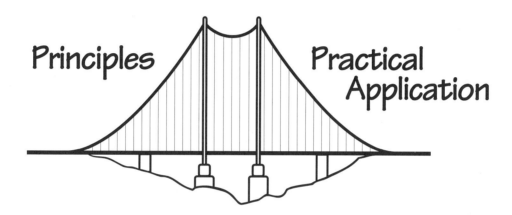

Our pastor recently sent out as a Christmas gift to all families in the parish a wonderful book, *The Christian Home*, written by Rev. Celestine Strub, O.F.M., in 1934. The author talks about the importance of families keeping a budget in the following way:

"The best way for parents to avoid excessive or ill-advised expenditures is to keep a family budget. Let them make a careful study of their resources and a classified list of their needs; e.g., housing, food, clothing, running expenses, improvement, and savings. Then let them fix a certain percentage of their income for each of these items of expense, and hold their disbursements strictly within the budget allowance, unless real necessity or charity require otherwise. Keeping a home and a family is just as much a business as running a store; so why should it not be kept on a business basis? Many couples have had their eyes opened by keeping an itemized account of disbursements. They found that they had been extravagant without realizing it. But if keeping tab on one's expenses teaches economy, it should be done in every Christian home; for economy, supernaturalized, is nothing but the Christian virtue of moderation."

If keeping a home was just as much a business as running a store in 1934, it is certainly *more* so now with such things as variable rate mortgages, complex insurance and investment options, automatic teller machines, credit cards, and a tax system that's nearly impossible to understand.

What would happen if you tried to take a cross country vacation without the benefit of a map or if you ignored warning signs, like WRONG WAY and DANGER and STOP? You would probably never reach your destination — or worse, you might end up in a crash. Trying to manage family finances without a basic financial plan is no different. Unfortunately, statistics tell us that upwards of 95 percent of families don't use a budget, which is the map of financial planning. When we haven't taken the time to properly plan our course, we shouldn't be surprised when a "financial wreck" occurs.

Families who veer so close to the edge financially, who have little savings and excessive debt, often resort to the quick fix of credit cards or other loans when any little bump in the road occurs. What they don't realize is that with 20-percent interest rates, such borrowing digs a financial hole that can be difficult to climb out of.

Anxiety and worry from these financial pressures often cripple communication between husband and wife. They desperately wish the problem would just go away, and they are baffled as to how to solve it. Some resort to bankruptcy, but find that without a change in both their attitude and their habits, they often fall back into financial bondage.

I want you to know there is hope. When the principles found in Sacred Scripture and the Teaching and Tradition of the Holy Catholic Church are applied in a practical way to your finances, the anxiety and worry that once plagued this area of your lives can turn into peace and contentment. There's no better time to get started than right now, so let's begin.

Tools of the Trade

The family financial toolbox consists of six basic tools, two of which I consider primary and four more which are supporting:

Primary

- Balance Sheet

- Budget Worksheet

Supporting

- Summary of Debts

- Checkbook Register

- Individual Account Register

- Guideline Budget

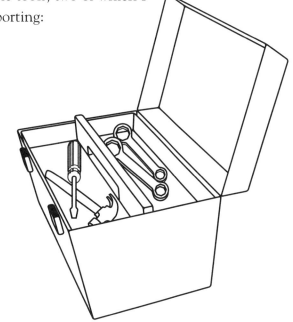

We'll learn about these tools by visiting with the Stewarts, a fictitious family that represents the common issues I see in my counseling. Before we can start, a little background is needed about these basic tools.

Balance Sheet and Budget Worksheet (Primary Tools)

The balance sheet and budget worksheet are two of the primary tools of financial planning. The balance sheet summarizes your assets and liabilities, while the budget worksheet summarizes your income and expenses. You can think of the balance sheet as a "snapshot" of your current financial position and your budget worksheet as a "video" of your finances over the last year.

Key components of the balance sheet include:

- Liquid assets (those that are immediately available as cash), such as your checking account and money market savings accounts.

- Invested assets such as certificates of deposit, mutual funds, retirement plans or other business investments.

- Other assets such as your house, automobiles, and home furnishings.

- Liabilities, which consist of all debts, including the mortgage on the house, home equity loans, automobile loans, credit-card debts, and any business-related debts.

- Net worth, which equals assets minus liabilities.

29

Key components of the budget worksheet include:

- Columns for both actual and budgeted income and expenses. The budget column works best when a one-year period is used to measure income and expenses. This makes it much easier to capture periodic expenses such as property taxes, insurance, holidays, and vacations. It also assists someone whose income fluctuates throughout the year (commission based sales people for example) to smooth out the effect of those fluctuations.

- Columns for both dollars and percentages help you better analyze your situation.

- The form has been broken down into fifteen main categories, one for income and fourteen for spending.

- Each of the fifteen categories has multiple sub-categories to help you see more clearly where your money is coming from and where it is going.

- The bottom of the form includes a section summarizing your total income and expenses. When your income exceeds your expenses, this is shown by a positive amount; if your expenses exceed your income, it is shown by a negative amount.

- The form emphasizes almsgiving/tithing, the education of children and saving by placing these categories at the top after income and taxes.

Until your family's financial information is summarized using these forms, it is virtually impossible to know where you've *been*, let alone where you are *going*. Once you have this information at your fingertips, husband and wife (or the single head of household) can begin reviewing the status of their finances and start planning for the future. Through the proper use of these forms and the right attitude, what used to be an area of poor communication for couples can become one of the best. Your confidence rises as you begin to establish your family's financial priorities in accord with God's word.

Supporting Tools

The supporting forms are the building blocks which provide the information you need to complete your balance sheet and budget worksheet. Let's take a look at how these work.

Summary of Debts

The summary of debts is a supporting schedule for the balance sheet. This form provides all of the critical information relating to your debts — whom the money is owed to, current balance, number of payments remaining, interest rate, and the minimum payment required. This worksheet becomes very helpful if you are dealing with extensive credit problems.

Checkbook Register

The checkbook register is the original source for the actual expenses that you see on the budget worksheet. This is where all of your checks, automatic teller machine withdrawals, deposits, and other banking activities are documented. But the information isn't organized in a way that lets you see how you are progressing according to your plan. That's where the individual account register comes in.

Individual Account Register

The individual account register is used to summarize your checkbook activity by the categories used on the budget worksheet. A separate account sheet is used for each sub-category that applies to your family. You can see that the form has columns for the date, check number, description, amount, and cumulative total. The amount in the cumulative total column is what gets transferred to the budget worksheet. I have found that using a cumulative total throughout the year, rather than looking at each month separately, provides the most accurate picture of a family's income and expenses.

Guideline Budget

Many families have a difficult time setting up a budget initially, because they have not previously tracked their expenses. As a result, they really have no idea what amounts to include in the various categories. To help overcome this problem, we have developed a guideline budget that can be used as a family's starter budget.

The guideline budget is only meant to help you get started. After you have successfully tracked your expenses for a few months, you will be in a position to develop your *own* budget, which will take into account your special circumstances and priorities. It is not important that your spending agree with the guideline in every area, but it is *critical* that your expenses not exceed your income.

Just as important is that our priorities reflect our Catholic faith. Therefore, tithing/almsgiving, education and savings are all given high priorities and planned for as any other expense.

Guideline Budget — Family of Six

	$	%	$	%	$	%
Gross Income	30,000	100	50,000	100	70,000	100
Less:						
Tithe	3,000	10	5,000	10	7,000	10
Taxes	3,700	12	7,500	15	13,200	19
Education	1,500	5	2,500	5	3,500	5
Savings	1,200	4	3,500	7	5,600	8
Housing	9,000	30	14,000	28	19,600	28
Groceries	5,000	17	6,000	12	6,400	9
Automobile	3,000	10	5,000	10	5,600	8
Medical	900	3	1,500	3	2,100	3
Insurance	900	3	1,500	3	2,100	3
Debt Payments	0	0	0	0	0	0
Clothing	600	2	1,500	3	2,100	3
Entertain./Recreation	600	2	1,500	3	1,400	2
Work Related	-	-	-	-	-	-
Miscellaneous	600	2	1,000	2	1,400	2
Total Expenses	30,000	100	50,000	100	70,000	100

Time for the Stewart Family's Annual Financial Physical

Jim and Nancy Stewart are in their late thirties and have four children ranging from 1 to 14 years of age. Jim has a good job as a middle manager of a small manufacturing company with an annual salary of $50,000 and Nancy is a full-time homemaker. They have never really learned how to manage their money, and they have never established any specific financial goals.

They have basically lived month to month, and when there was a little too much month left at the end of the money, they relied on credit cards to get them through. Their oldest child is reaching college age, and they don't have a plan to assist with college expenses. They realize that they aren't getting any younger and that they need to look toward providing for their retirement. With all this in mind, let's take a look at the Stewarts finances using the tools mentioned above.

When a family asks for financial counseling, the first thing I do is send a package to them consisting of the balance sheet, summary of debts, budget worksheet, and guideline budget. I ask that they make a first pass at completing the forms. This effort is meant to be a rough estimate of what is really happening, and should only take an hour or two. I ask them to do the following:

Balance Sheet and Summary of Debts

List amounts for all assets and liabilities as of the most recent date. For example, use today's balance in the check register and balances from the most recent bank statements for savings accounts and investments. List the current value of your home, car, and home furnishings, and then enter the sum of all assets on the line titled "Total Assets." For liabilities, begin with the summary of debts by listing all of the requested information related to each loan. This information should be available on the monthly statements from your lenders. If not, contact your lender to determine the necessary information. Once you have completed the summary of debts, transfer the amounts to the balance sheet by category of debt (mortgage, home equity loan, auto loan, credit card debt, etc.). The sum of these should be entered on the line "Total Liabilities." Total assets minus total liabilities equals net worth and should be entered on that line.

Budget Worksheet and Guideline Budget

- Write down your estimated annual income, using the same amounts for the actual column and the budget column.

- From the guideline budget table, find the column closest to your income level. Take the appropriate percentage from each of the main spending categories and write this percentage in the budget percentage column.

- Multiply the guideline budget percentage by the annual income dollar amount. This provides the guideline budget dollars for each main spending category.

- Estimate your actual annual spending for each of the sub-categories and write the amounts on the appropriate line under the actual amount column.

- Add the actual amounts listed in each sub-category and write the total on the main category line.

- Divide the actual amount for each main category by your total estimated gross income (before taxes) and write the percentage in the actual percentage column.

- Complete the summary in the lower right-hand corner. Now you can compare what you think you're spending to our guideline budget.

Let's Visit with the Stewart Family

Balance Sheet and Summary of Debts

Jim and Nancy did a good job of completing their forms. In reviewing the balance sheet (Exhibit 1a), you can see that their most significant asset is their house. With the exception of Jim's retirement plan from work, they have very little in the way of cash or investments. Their other assets consist of two cars and their home furnishings.

Jim and Nancy's liabilities consist of their mortgage, one auto loan, and credit card debts. You can see that they owe $10,000 on credit cards, which are documented in greater detail on the summary of debts form (Exhibit 1b). The balance sheet shows the Stewarts have a net worth of $68,100.

Budget Worksheet and Guideline Budget

In reviewing the summary of income and expenses on the budget worksheet (Exhibit 1c), you can see that the Stewart family is estimating that their annual expenses exceed their income by $2,000, or 4% of their income.

By comparing the guideline budget percentages to the actual percentages, we can determine which areas are most out of line and should be looked into. For the Stewarts, the most significant differences show up in the categories of tithing/almsgiving, taxes, savings, housing, groceries, debt payments, clothing, entertainment and recreation and miscellaneous.

Balance Sheet as of December 31 — Exhibit 1a

Description	Amount
Assets	
Liquid Assets	
Cash on Hand	100
Cash — Checking	1,000
Cash — Money Market	-
Cash — Other Available	-
Invested Assets	
Certificates of Deposit	-
Mutual Funds, Stocks and Bonds	-
Retirement Plan	12,000
Business Investment	-
Other Assets	
House	150,000
Autos	15,000
Other	10,000
Total Assets	**188,100**
Liabilities	
House Mortgage	100,000
Home Equity Loan	-
Auto Loans	10,000
Credit Card Liabilities	10,000
Business Debt	-
Total Liabilities	**120,000**
Net Worth	**68,100**

Summary of Debts as of December 31 — Exhibit 1b

To Whom Owed	Balance Due	# of Payments Remaining	Interest Rate	Minimum Required Payment
Name: First National Bank Address: 1000 Main Street City: Anytown USA State: Small State Zip: 11111 Account #12345 Contact Person: Mr. Smith Telephone#: 111-1111	100,000	240	7%	800
Name: Second National Bank Address: 2000 Main Street City: Anytown USA State: Small State Zip: 11111 Account #12345 Contact Person: Mr. Smith Telephone#: 222-2222	10,000	60	10%	200
Name: Third National Bank Address: 3000 Main Street City: Anytown USA State: Small State Zip: 11111 Account #12345 Contact Person: Mr. Smith Telephone#: 333-3333	4,000	Credit Card	19%	150
Name: Fourth National Bank Address: 4000 Main Street City: Anytown USA State: Small State Zip: 11111 Account #12345 Contact Person: Mr. Smith Telephone#: 444-4444	4,000	Credit Card	19%	150
Name: Fifth National Bank Address: 5000 Main Street City: Anytown USA State: Small State Zip: 11111 Account #12345 Contact Person: Mr. Smith Telephone#: 555-5555	2,000	Credit Card	19%	75

"To the Greater Glory of God ~ Ad Majorem Dei Gloriam"

Budget Worksheet as of December 31 — Exhibit 1c

Account Description	To Date Actual $	To Date Actual %	Annual Budget $	Annual Budget %
Gross Income	50,000	100%	50,000	100%
Salary	48,000			
Bonus				
Interest	100			
Dividends				
Retirement Plan	1,900			
Other Investment Income				
Other				
Tithing/Almsgiving	500	1%	5,000	10%
Deductible	300			
Non-deductible	100			
Faith Education	100			
Taxes	8,500	17%	7,500	15%
Federal Income	3,400			
State Income	1,100			
Social Security	3,000			
Medicare	800			
State Disability	200			
Other				
Current Education	2,500	5%	2,500	5%
Tuition	1,500			
Materials	500			
Transportation				
Other	500			
Savings	2,000	4%	3,500	7%
Contingency	100			
Future Education				
Retirement	1,900			
Housing	15,000	30%	14,000	28%
Mortgage/Rent	9,600			
Insurance	600			
Taxes	1,300			
Electricity	600			
Gas	400			
Water	400			
Gardening	700			
Housecleaning				
Telephone	700			
Maintenance	200			
Pest Control				
Association Dues				
Bottled Water				
Improvements	500			
Other				
Groceries	7,000	14%	6,000	12%

Budget Worksheet as of December 31 (Continued)

Account Description	To Date Actual $	To Date Actual %	Annual Budget $	Annual Budget %
Automobile	4,500	9%	5,000	10%
Payments	2,400			
Gas/Oil	700			
Insurance	700			
License/Taxes	300			
Maintenance/Repair	400			
Other				
Medical Expenses	1,500	3%	1,500	3%
Doctor	750			
Dentist	500			
Prescriptions	250			
Other				
Insurance	1,500	3%	1,500	3%
Life	750			
Medical	250			
Disability	500			
Other				
Debt Payments	2,500	5%	-	-
Credit Card	2,500			
Loans and Notes				
Other				
Clothing	2,500	5%	1,500	3%
Entertain. and Recreation	2,000	4%	1,000	2%
Eating Out	800			
Child Care				
Allowances				
Activites	200			
Vacation	700			
Cable Television/Movies	250			
Other	50			
Work Related	-	-	-	-
Education/Dues				
Clothing				
Child Care				
Other				
Miscellaneous	2,000	4%	1,000	2%
Beauty/Barber/Cosmetics	750			
Laundry	100			
Subscriptions	200			
Holidays	800			
Home Expenses	150			
Veterinarian				
Other				
Summary of Inc./Exp.				
Total Income	50,000	100%	50,000	100%
Total Expenses	52,000	104%	50,000	100%
Income Over/(Under) Exp.	(2,000)	(4%)	-	-

Tracking Expenses and the Individual Account Register

At the end of the first meeting, the Stewarts were given the assignment to begin tracking their expenses using the individual account register. Remember, they had completed the budget worksheet by estimating their annual expenses and comparing them to the guideline budget. Now they will track their expenses to verify that their estimates were accurate. After a few months of tracking their activity, they will be in a position to develop a budget that has been customized for their own family's circumstances.

It's time for our next visit with the Stewarts. Let's see how they did. The budget worksheet (Exhibit 2a) shows that the Stewarts have income from Mr. Stewart's job (salary), as well as interest and retirement plan income. Therefore, they have three separate individual account registers for income. Exhibit 2b shows the individual account register for Jim's salary for the first three months of the year. The same concept applies for the spending categories. Under the automobile category, the Stewarts show expenses for car payments, gas and oil, insurance, licenses, and maintenance. Therefore, they used five individual account registers to track spending in this area. Exhibits 2c, d, and e show the individual account registers for gas and oil, insurance, and maintenance.

"To the Greater Glory of God ~ Ad Majorem Dei Gloriam"

Budget Worksheet as of March 31 — Exhibit 2a

Account Description	To Date Actual $	To Date Actual %	Annual Budget $	Annual Budget %
Gross Income	12,500	100%	50,000	100%
Salary	12,000			
Bonus				
Interest	25			
Dividends				
Retirement Plan	475			
Other Investment Income				
Other				
Tithing/Almsgiving	125	1%	5,000	10%
Deductible	75			
Non-deductible	25			
Faith Education	25			
Taxes	2,125	17%	7,500	15%
Federal Income	850			
State Income	275			
Social Security	750			
Medicare	200			
State Disability	50			
Other				
Current Education	625	5%	2,500	5%
Tuition	375			
Materials	125			
Transportation				
Other	125			
Savings	500	4%	3,500	7%
Contingency	25			
Future Education				
Retirement	475			
Housing	3,750	30%	14,000	28%
Mortgage/Rent	2,400			
Insurance	175			
Taxes	325			
Electricity	150			
Gas	100			
Water	100			
Gardening	175			
Housecleaning				
Telephone	700			
Maintenance	50			
Pest Control				
Association Dues				
Bottled Water				
Improvements	125			
Other				
Groceries	1,750	14%	6,000	12%

Budget Worksheet as of March 31 (Continued)

Account Description	To Date Actual $	To Date Actual %	Annual Budget $	Annual Budget %
Automobile	1,125	9%	5,000	10%
Payments	600			
Gas/Oil	200			
Insurance	200			
License/Taxes				
Maintenance/Repair	125			
Other				
Medical Expenses	375	3%	1,500	3%
Doctor	187			
Dentist	125			
Prescriptions	63			
Other				
Insurance	375	3%	1,500	3%
Life	187			
Medical	63			
Disability	125			
Other				
Debt Payments	625	5%	-	-
Credit Card	625			
Loans and Notes				
Other				
Clothing	625	5%	1,500	3%
Entertain. and Recreation	500	4%	1,000	2%
Eating Out	200			
Child Care				
Allowances				
Activites	50			
Vacation	175			
Cable Television/Movies	63			
Other	12			
Work Related	-	-	-	-
Education/Dues				
Clothing				
Child Care				
Other				
Miscellaneous	500	4%	1,000	2%
Beauty/Barber/Cosmetics	200			
Laundry	25			
Subscriptions	50			
Holidays	175			
Home Expenses	50			
Veterinarian				
Other				
Summary of Inc./Exp.				
Total Income	12,500	100%	50,000	100%
Total Expenses	13,000	104%	50,000	100%
Income Over/(Under) Exp.	(500)	(4%)	-	-

Individual Account Register
Account Description: Salary — Annual Budget: 48,000

Date	Check #	Description	Amount	Cumulative Total
1/31/X4	101	January Paycheck	4,000.00	4,000.00
2/28/X4	201	February Paycheck	4,000.00	8,000.00
3/31/X4	301	March Paycheck	4,000.00	12,000.00

Individual Account Register
Account Description: Gas/Oil   Annual Budget: 800

Date	Check #	Description	Amount	Cumulative Total
1/4/X4	1023	Gas Card	65.00	65.00
2/4/X4	1063	Gas Card	70.00	135.00
3/4/X4	1093	Gas Card	65.00	200.00

Individual Account Register

Account Description: Automobile Insurance   Annual Budget: 800

Date	Check #	Description	Amount	Cumulative Total
2/15X4	1045	Insurance Company	200.00	200.00

Individual Account Register
Account Description: Automobile Maintenance   Annual Budget: 1,000

Date	Check #	Description	Amount	Cumulative Total
3/14/X4	1075	Joe's Auto shop	100.00	100.00
3/21/X4	1086	Oil Change Shop	25.00	125.00

What's Next?

Now that the Stewarts have faithfully tracked their expenses for three months, it's time for them to establish their own budget. They now have sufficient information to develop a plan that will allow them to bring their finances into alignment with the principles in Sacred Scripture and Church Teaching. Specifically, they will work towards increasing their tithe to the full 10 percent, eliminating their credit card debts, and reviewing other spending areas so that overall spending does not exceed the available income.

Communication between husband and wife is critical at this point. The Stewarts decided to get a baby-sitter for a few hours so they could go to a quiet place and talk about their family's financial priorities. Using their latest balance sheet and budget worksheet, they discussed the following issues:

- After studying the principles to guide family finances, they decided to increase their tithe from 1 percent to 10 percent. This was a serious decision for the Stewarts because their spending already exceeded their income by 4 percent. To bring spending in line with income after they began tithing, they had to increase income or reduce spending by 13 percent! However, they were convinced that this was what God was calling them to do.

- As a result of their tithing decision, they now have increased deductions for tax purposes, resulting in a lower tax liability.

- Savings for contingencies has been increased to 5% which is below the guideline of 7%, but for the next three years, the Stewarts will focus on reducing debt, then they will increase their savings to at least the guideline level.

- They made a commitment to eliminate their credit card debt and to use credit cards in the future *only if they paid for the current month's purchases in full each month*. Otherwise, they would cut the cards up and cancel them.

- In the housing category, the Stewarts shopped around for homeowner's insurance and found they could save $100. They had hired a gardener a year before, and they decided to go back to doing the yard work themselves for an additional $500 in savings. They also reduced their spending on improvements by $300.

- In the groceries category, the Stewarts realized they were purchasing a lot of prepackaged foods, which added significantly to their spending. By purchasing staples in larger quantities and preparing their own food, they were able to reduce spending in this category by $700.

- The Stewarts had recently purchased a new car and financed about half of the purchase price. They realized now that this was a mistake and that, to bring their budget into balance, they would need to sell the new car and replace it with a used one so they could use these resources on eliminating their credit card debt.

- The Stewarts had been shopping for clothing at the trendier department stores. They realize they can save money if they shop carefully and focus more on handing down clothes for the younger children. They believe they can save $1,000.

- In the area of entertainment and recreation, the Stewarts realize they need to cut back on eating out, which has become a twice-a-week event. They will also eliminate the cable television. Instead of expensive outings, they will work on planning less costly family activities, such as picnics, camping, etc. They estimate reducing spending in this area by $1,000.

- In the miscellaneous category, the Stewarts agreed to begin cutting the hair of the youngest children themselves, eliminating their subscriptions and using the library instead, and reducing their holiday spending by $300. Total estimated savings amount to $1,000.

- Jim was fortunate to receive an 8% raise shortly after they began the counseling program and this has been factored into their new budget.

Three Years Later . . .

Convinced that God was calling them to be diligent in the area of their family finances, Jim and Nancy continued to track their expenses and maintain their budget. You can see the results of their efforts by reviewing exhibits 3a, b, and c.

- They have eliminated their credit card debt!

- Now they are in a position to use the $5,000 that was going to creditors in other ways. They have agreed to apply most of it to savings to be used for college expenses and a new car. The remainder will pay for a family vacation which has been well earned!

- The biggest impact on the Stewarts has been the change in attitude. By submitting their finances to the principles outlined in Sacred Scripture and the Teaching and Tradition of the Catholic Church, they have come to know a peace and contentment that had not been possible before. What used to be one of the most difficult areas of their marriage has been turned into one of the best!

Balance Sheet as of December 31 — Exhibit 3a

Description	Amount
Assets	
Liquid Assets	
Cash on Hand	100
Cash — Checking	3,500
Cash — Money Market	-
Cash — Other Available	-
Invested Assets	
Certificates of Deposit	-
Mutual Funds, Stocks and Bonds	-
Retirement Plan	20,000
Business Investment	-
Other Assets	
House	150,000
Autos	10,000
Other	10,000
Total Assets	**193,600**
Liabilities	
House Mortgage	90,000
Home Equity Loan	-
Auto Loans	-
Credit Card Liabilities	-
Business Debt	-
Total Liabilities	**90,000**
Net Worth	**103,600**

Summary of Debts as of December 31 — Exhibit 3b

To Whom Owed	Balance Due	# of Payments Remaining	Interest Rate	Minimum Required Payment
Name: First National Bank Address: 1000 Main Street City: Anytown USA State: Small State Zip: 11111 Account #12345 Contact Person: Mr. Smith Telephone#: 111-1111	90,000	204	7%	800
Name: Second National Bank Address: 2000 Main Street City: Anytown USA State: Small State Zip: 11111 Account #12345 Contact Person: Mr. Smith Telephone#: 222-2222	-	-	10%	-
Name: Third National Bank Address: 3000 Main Street City: Anytown USA State: Small State Zip: 11111 Account #12345 Contact Person: Mr. Smith Telephone#: 333-3333	-	Credit Card	19%	-
Name: Fourth National Bank Address: 4000 Main Street City: Anytown USA State: Small State Zip: 11111 Account #12345 Contact Person: Mr. Smith Telephone#: 444-4444	-	Credit Card	19%	-
Name: Fifth National Bank Address: 5000 Main Street City: Anytown USA State: Small State Zip: 11111 Account #12345 Contact Person: Mr. Smith Telephone#: 555-5555	-	Credit Card	19%	-

Budget Worksheet as of December 31 — Exhibit 3c

Account Description	To Date Actual $	To Date Actual %	Annual Budget $	Annual Budget %
Gross Income	54,000	100%	54,000	100%
Salary	52,000		52,000	
Bonus				
Interest	100		100	
Dividends				
Retirement Plan	1,900		1,900	
Other Investment Income				
Other				
Tithing/Almsgiving	5,400	10%	5,400	10%
Deductible	3,200		3,200	
Non-deductible	1,100		1,100	
Faith Education	1,100		1,100	
Taxes	8,300	15%	8,300	15%
Federal Income	2,900		2,900	
State Income	1,100		1,100	
Social Security	3,100		3,100	
Medicare	900		900	
State Disability	300		300	
Other				
Current Education	2,500	5%	2,500	5%
Tuition	1,500		1,500	
Materials	500		500	
Transportation				
Other	500		500	
Savings	2,700	5%	2,700	5%
Contingency	800		800	
Future Education				
Retirement	1,900		1,900	
Housing	14,300	26%	14,300	26%
Mortgage/Rent	9,600		9,600	
Insurance	500		500	
Taxes	1,300		1,300	
Electricity	600		600	
Gas	600		600	
Water	400		400	
Gardening	200		200	
Housecleaning				
Telephone	700		700	
Maintenance	200		200	
Pest Control				
Association Dues				
Bottled Water				
Improvements	200		200	
Other				
Groceries	6,300	11%	6,300	11%

Account Description	To Date Actual $	To Date Actual %	Annual Budget $	Annual Budget %
Automobile	3,000	6%	3,000	6%
Payments				
Gas/Oil	800		800	
Insurance	800		800	
License/Taxes	400		400	
Maintenance/Repair	1,000		1,000	
Other				
Medical Expenses	1,500	3%	1,500	3%
Doctor	750		750	
Dentist	500		500	
Prescriptions	250		250	
Other				
Insurance	1,500	3%	1,500	3%
Life	750		750	
Medical	250		250	
Disability	500		500	
Other				
Debt Payments	5,000	9%	5,000	9%
Credit Card	5,000		5,000	
Loans and Notes				
Other				
Clothing	1,500	3%	1,500	3%
Entertain. and Recreation	1,000	2%	1,000	2%
Eating Out	250		250	
Child Care				
Allowances				
Activites	250		250	
Vacation	500		500	
Cable Television/Movies				
Other				
Work Related	-	-	-	-
Education/Dues				
Clothing				
Child Care				
Other				
Miscellaneous	1,000	2%	1,000	2%
Beauty/Barber/Cosmetics	450		450	
Laundry				
Subscriptions				
Holidays	500		500	
Home Expenses	50		50	
Veterinarian				
Other				
Summary of Inc./Exp.				
Total Income	54,000	100%	54,000	100%
Total Expenses	54,000	100%	54,000	100%
Income Over/(Under) Exp.	-	-	-	-

You Can Do It Too!

Now that you've seen how the Stewart family applied the financial tools to their situation, it's time for you to do the same. In this chapter, we'll summarize the steps you need to take and provide some additional tips that will help you succeed. Master forms have been provided for your use at the end of the book.

Step #1 — Determine Where You Are

Set aside a couple of hours away from distractions when you and your spouse are both well rested (this is important!), and make a first pass at completing the balance sheet, summary of debts, and budget worksheet.

Remember, as you complete the budget worksheet, that you are only estimating your annual income and expenses at this point. This entire effort should take no more than two hours. If you have questions on how to complete the forms, review the case of the Stewart family.

What did you find out about your finances as a result of completing the forms? How did your spending patterns match up with the guideline budget? Does the summary of debts show extensive credit problems? Does the budget worksheet show expenses exceeding income by a significant amount?

If so, *don't despair*. Once you clearly see the issues you are dealing with and make a commitment to follow the principles we have discussed, you can deal with virtually *any* financial issues confronting your family.

Step #2 — Track Your Expenses

In order to verify that the amounts you estimated for income and expenses are accurate, begin tracking your expenses by each sub-category on the budget worksheet. Once again, if you have questions, refer to the example of the Stewart family. At the end of the month, you will use the cumulative total on this schedule to update your budget worksheet.

Step #3 — Update the Balance Sheet, Summary of Debts and Budget Worksheet Monthly

At the end of each month, update your balance sheet, summary of debts and budget worksheet. How do your actual expense percentages compare to your initial estimate? Because certain expenses don't occur evenly every month, it may take a few months of tracking your actual income and expenses before you'll be able to make a good comparison to your original estimates.

Step #4 — Develop Your Customized Budget

Once you have tracked your income and expenses for a few months, you have sufficient information to develop your own budget. At this point, husband and wife should set aside a couple of hours where they can have some quiet time to develop their plan.

This is the time that you turn the principles we have discussed into a real way of life for your family. It's where you develop a plan that will help you "live your faith through your finances."

Families who have successfully completed the steps up to this point will have financial situations ranging from comfortable to urgent. If you find that your finances are in good shape, which means you have savings for a rainy day, no credit card or other consumer debt, an overall positive net worth, and a balanced budget, I applaud you. You now have the tools and the knowledge to insure continued success in this area.

If, on the other hand, you find that your balance sheet shows significant consumer debts and inadequate savings, or that your expenses exceed your income, it's time to develop a plan that puts you on solid ground financially.

Just as with the Stewart family, you may need to make decisions as a family that are not easy. But you'll find that the peace and contentment that comes with living within your means and applying God's principles to your finances far outweigh the short term pain of cutting back. If you find you need to make adjustments to your spending, discuss your priorities *as a couple* and come to a mutual decision on areas to be affected. If you have older children or teenagers, you will want to ask for their ideas, too - although the final decisions, of course, must be made by the adults.

Additional Tips

Adopt a Proactive Attitude

One of the most significant factors which will influence your success in *taking control* of your family finances is a proactive attitude. Let's take a look at what Sacred Scripture and Church Teaching have to say about attitude. As always, Proverbs is filled with wisdom. Chapter 27:23 says, "Take good care of your flocks, give careful attention to your herds." In chapter 24:30–34, we read, "I passed by the field of the sluggard, by the vineyard of the man without sense; And behold! It was all overgrown with thistles; its surface was covered with nettles, and its stone wall broken down. And as I gazed at it, I reflected; I saw and learned the lesson: A little sleep, a little slumber, a little folding of the arms to rest — then will poverty come upon you like a highwayman, and want like an armed man."

If you want your finances well organized, a certain level of commitment is required. However, as you see the benefits of reduced frustration and anxiety, I think you'll agree the commitment is worth it.

Build an Orderly File System

Once you've committed to getting organized, the next step is to establish a filing system for all of the paperwork that comes your way (I keep hearing about a paperless society, but I haven't seen it yet!).

I recommend that your files be broken down into two main categories: *current* and *long-term*. Since you will refer to your current files frequently, the system works best if they are accessible where you pay bills, such as a file drawer in a desk or a file cabinet close by. On the other hand, you will not need to refer to your long term files very often so they could be kept in a file cabinet in the garage.

I have found that hanging folders with manila folder inserts work very well for home files. You can find inexpensive plastic crates or portable files that will hold these quite well if you can't afford a filing cabinet.

You can use the following list as a starting point for your own files, but don't be afraid to customize them to fit your own circumstances.

Current Files

- Open Items (bills to pay, unreconciled bank statements).

- Tithing/Almsgiving (church envelopes, correspondence).

- Taxes (current year pay stubs, W-2 and correspondence).

- Education (receipts, correspondence).

- Savings (separate folders for bank accounts, retirement plan, and other investments).

- Housing (separate folders for statements, property taxes and insurance).

- Automobile (separate folders for each car and insurance).

- Medical Records (separate folders for medical history, current year bills, and your policy).

- Insurance (separate folders for life and disability).

- Debt Payments (separate folders for each credit card or loan).

Long-Term Files

- Employment (employment handbook, résumé).

- Taxes (separate folders for each prior year).

- Savings (separate folders for prior year bank statements, retirement plan, and other investments).

- Housing (separate files for permanent items such as purchase documents, receipts for improvements, and prior-period property taxes).

- Social Security (separate folders for each family member).

- Estate Planning (separate folders for copies of your will or trust and those of other family members as appropriate).

Manage That Checkbook!

When you're at the checkout counter of the grocery store ready to write your check with your baby wiggling in your arms, how often do you just give up on entering the check information in the register, saying you'll get to it when you get home? Then when you get home, all chaos breaks loose and before you know it, you can't remember how much the check was for? For the person who handles the checkbook responsibilities, the frustration level rises as they try to reconstruct what happened.

One of the greatest inventions in the last few years that can go a long way toward eliminating this friction between a husband and wife are carbon-copy checks. When you write the check at the store, an automatic copy remains in your checkbook that can be used to update your register later. I highly recommend them.

It is critical that you reconcile your checkbook each month when your bank statement arrives. Use the following steps:

- Match all withdrawals and deposits on the bank statement to your check register. Use a check mark in your register to document that the item has been matched. Don't forget to include all ATM and pre-authorized transactions. If any of your documentation doesn't match with the bank's information after double checking, call the bank.

- Document any fees or other charges the bank has made in your checkbook.

- Most bank statements provide a form for reconciling the account on the reverse side of the statement.

- Develop your deposit in transit by listing all deposits that appear in your checkbook which do not appear on your bank statement.

- Develop your outstanding withdrawals by listing all withdrawals that appear in your checkbook which do not appear on the bank statement.

Bank statement ending balance + deposits in transit – outstanding withdrawals = Checkbook balance. If the total matches your checkbook total, congratulations, you have successfully balanced your checkbook! If it doesn't, retrace your steps asking yourself:

- Did I make an addition or subtraction error in my checkbook or my list of deposits-in-transit or outstanding withdrawals?

- Did I miss recording a transaction in the checkbook? (Do a quick review by check number.)

- Did I properly list outstanding items that carried over from the prior month's reconciliation?

If after these steps you still don't reconcile, you may want to call your bank for guidance.

Develop a Regular "Maintenance" Schedule

In our counseling program, we meet with a couple once a month for several months. As we sit down to discuss how they are doing, I can often see that they were up late the night before finishing their paperwork.

Rather than having the financial planning process be a fire drill each month, I encourage you to take time each week to pay bills and log your expenses. We have found that by taking just an additional ten minutes each week, we avoid that big buildup of paperwork that can be so depressing to deal with. I strongly urge you to establish a fixed time each week to pay bills and track your expenses. Make it a coffee date!

Weekly (Paying bills, updating your checkbook and individual account register)
Make sure you have all of the supplies you will need such as your checkbook, envelopes, a pen, postage stamps, return-address stamp, calculator, and your Financial Organizer binder.

Retrieve all of your bills to pay from your "open bills" file. Review them for accuracy and prioritize them for payment. If not due until after your next bill paying session (including sufficient mailing time), place back in open bills file.

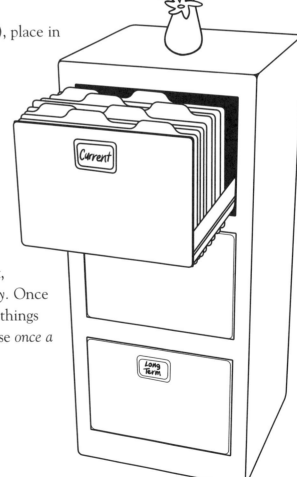

Write the checks (don't forget to sign them!), place in the envelopes, stamp and mail.

Document your expenditures in your check register and on the appropriate individual account register in your Financial Organizer. Mark the checkbook register with a special checkmark to note that the amount has been transferred to your organizer.

Monthly
Until you have your finances in order, I recommend that you update your balance sheet, summary of debts and budget worksheet *monthly*. Once you have established a solid financial plan and things are running smoothly, you can then update these *once a quarter*.

In Closing...

It is my hope and prayer that, as your family applies the principles and tools found in this guide, you experience the joy of submitting your finances to the Kingship of Christ. If we can be of any further assistance, please contact us. God love you!

Balance Sheet as of _____

Description   Amount

Assets

Liquid Assets

Cash on Hand   _____

Cash — Checking   _____

Cash — Money Market   _____

Cash — Other Available   _____

Invested Assets

Certificates of Deposit   _____

Mutual Funds, Stocks and Bonds   _____

Retirement Plan   _____

Business Investment   _____

Other Assets

House   _____

Autos   _____

Other   _____

Total Assets   _____

Liabilities

House Mortgage   _____

Home Equity Loan   _____

Auto Loans   _____

Credit Card Liabilities   _____

Business Debt   _____

Total Liabilities   _____

Net Worth   _____

Balance Sheet as of _____

Description   Amount

Assets

Liquid Assets

Cash on Hand   _____

Cash — Checking   _____

Cash — Money Market   _____

Cash — Other Available   _____

Invested Assets

Certificates of Deposit   _____

Mutual Funds, Stocks and Bonds   _____

Retirement Plan   _____

Business Investment   _____

Other Assets

House   _____

Autos   _____

Other   _____

Total Assets

_____

Liabilities

House Mortgage   _____

Home Equity Loan   _____

Auto Loans   _____

Credit Card Liabilities   _____

Business Debt   _____

Total Liabilities

_____

Net Worth

_____

Balance Sheet as of _____

Description   Amount

Assets

Liquid Assets

Cash on Hand   _____

Cash — Checking   _____

Cash — Money Market   _____

Cash — Other Available   _____

Invested Assets

Certificates of Deposit   _____

Mutual Funds, Stocks and Bonds   _____

Retirement Plan   _____

Business Investment   _____

Other Assets

House   _____

Autos   _____

Other   _____

Total Assets   _____

Liabilities

House Mortgage   _____

Home Equity Loan   _____

Auto Loans   _____

Credit Card Liabilities   _____

Business Debt   _____

Total Liabilities   _____

Net Worth   _____

Balance Sheet as of _____

Description   Amount

Assets

Liquid Assets

Cash on Hand   _____

Cash — Checking   _____

Cash — Money Market   _____

Cash — Other Available   _____

Invested Assets

Certificates of Deposit   _____

Mutual Funds, Stocks and Bonds   _____

Retirement Plan   _____

Business Investment   _____

Other Assets

House   _____

Autos   _____

Other   _____

Total Assets   _____

Liabilities

House Mortgage   _____

Home Equity Loan   _____

Auto Loans   _____

Credit Card Liabilities   _____

Business Debt   _____

Total Liabilities   _____

Net Worth   _____

"To the Greater Glory of God ~ Ad Majorem Dei Gloriam"

Balance Sheet as of _____

Description   Amount

Assets

Liquid Assets
Cash on Hand   _____
Cash — Checking   _____
Cash — Money Market   _____
Cash — Other Available   _____

Invested Assets
Certificates of Deposit   _____
Mutual Funds, Stocks and Bonds   _____
Retirement Plan   _____
Business Investment   _____

Other Assets
House   _____
Autos   _____
Other   _____

Total Assets   _____

Liabilities

House Mortgage   _____
Home Equity Loan   _____
Auto Loans   _____
Credit Card Liabilities   _____
Business Debt   _____

Total Liabilities   _____

Net Worth   _____

"To the Greater Glory of God ~ Ad Majorem Dei Gloriam"

Balance Sheet as of _____

Description   Amount

Assets

Liquid Assets

Cash on Hand   _____

Cash — Checking   _____

Cash — Money Market   _____

Cash — Other Available   _____

Invested Assets

Certificates of Deposit   _____

Mutual Funds, Stocks and Bonds   _____

Retirement Plan   _____

Business Investment   _____

Other Assets

House   _____

Autos   _____

Other   _____

Total Assets   _____

Liabilities

House Mortgage   _____

Home Equity Loan   _____

Auto Loans   _____

Credit Card Liabilities   _____

Business Debt   _____

Total Liabilities   _____

Net Worth   _____

Balance Sheet as of _____

Description	Amount

Assets

Liquid Assets
Cash on Hand _____
Cash — Checking _____
Cash — Money Market _____
Cash — Other Available _____

Invested Assets
Certificates of Deposit _____
Mutual Funds, Stocks and Bonds _____
Retirement Plan _____
Business Investment _____

Other Assets
House _____
Autos _____
Other _____

Total Assets _____

Liabilities

House Mortgage _____
Home Equity Loan _____
Auto Loans _____
Credit Card Liabilities _____
Business Debt _____

Total Liabilities _____

Net Worth _____

Balance Sheet as of _____

Description	Amount

Assets

Liquid Assets

Cash on Hand _____

Cash — Checking _____

Cash — Money Market _____

Cash — Other Available _____

Invested Assets

Certificates of Deposit _____

Mutual Funds, Stocks and Bonds _____

Retirement Plan _____

Business Investment _____

Other Assets

House _____

Autos _____

Other _____

Total Assets _____

Liabilities

House Mortgage _____

Home Equity Loan _____

Auto Loans _____

Credit Card Liabilities _____

Business Debt _____

Total Liabilities _____

Net Worth _____

Summary of Debts as of _____

To Whom Owed	Balance Due	# of Payments Remaining	Interest Rate	Minimum Required Payment
Name: _____ Address:_____ City: _____ State:_____ Zip: _____ Account # _____ Contact Person: _____ Telephone#: _____				
Name: _____ Address:_____ City: _____ State:_____ Zip: _____ Account # _____ Contact Person: _____ Telephone#: _____				
Name: _____ Address:_____ City: _____ State:_____ Zip: _____ Account # _____ Contact Person: _____ Telephone#: _____				
Name: _____ Address:_____ City: _____ State:_____ Zip: _____ Account # _____ Contact Person: _____ Telephone#: _____				
Name: _____ Address:_____ City: _____ State:_____ Zip: _____ Account # _____ Contact Person: _____ Telephone#: _____				

"To the Greater Glory of God ~ Ad Majorem Dei Gloriam"

Summary of Debts as of _____

To Whom Owed	Balance Due	# of Payments Remaining	Interest Rate	Minimum Required Payment
Name: _____ Address:_____ City: _____ State:_____ Zip: _____ Account #_____ Contact Person: _____ Telephone#: _____				
Name: _____ Address:_____ City: _____ State:_____ Zip: _____ Account #_____ Contact Person: _____ Telephone#: _____				
Name: _____ Address:_____ City: _____ State:_____ Zip: _____ Account #_____ Contact Person: _____ Telephone#: _____				
Name: _____ Address:_____ City: _____ State:_____ Zip: _____ Account #_____ Contact Person: _____ Telephone#: _____				
Name: _____ Address:_____ City: _____ State:_____ Zip: _____ Account #_____ Contact Person: _____ Telephone#: _____				

"To the Greater Glory of God ~ Ad Majorem Dei Gloriam"

Summary of Debts as of _____

To Whom Owed	Balance Due	# of Payments Remaining	Interest Rate	Minimum Required Payment
Name: _____ Address:_____ City: _____ State:_____ Zip: _____ Account # _____ Contact Person: _____ Telephone#: _____				
Name: _____ Address:_____ City: _____ State:_____ Zip: _____ Account # _____ Contact Person: _____ Telephone#: _____				
Name: _____ Address:_____ City: _____ State:_____ Zip: _____ Account # _____ Contact Person: _____ Telephone#: _____				
Name: _____ Address:_____ City: _____ State:_____ Zip: _____ Account # _____ Contact Person: _____ Telephone#: _____				
Name: _____ Address:_____ City: _____ State:_____ Zip: _____ Account # _____ Contact Person: _____ Telephone#: _____				

Summary of Debts as of _____

To Whom Owed	Balance Due	# of Payments Remaining	Interest Rate	Minimum Required Payment
Name: _____ Address:_____ City: _____ State:_____ Zip: _____ Account #_____ Contact Person: _____ Telephone#: _____				
Name: _____ Address:_____ City: _____ State:_____ Zip: _____ Account #_____ Contact Person: _____ Telephone#: _____				
Name: _____ Address:_____ City: _____ State:_____ Zip: _____ Account #_____ Contact Person: _____ Telephone#: _____				
Name: _____ Address:_____ City: _____ State:_____ Zip: _____ Account #_____ Contact Person: _____ Telephone#: _____				
Name: _____ Address:_____ City: _____ State:_____ Zip: _____ Account #_____ Contact Person: _____ Telephone#: _____				

Summary of Debts as of _____

To Whom Owed	Balance Due	# of Payments Remaining	Interest Rate	Minimum Required Payment
Name: _____ Address:_____ City: _____ State:_____ Zip: _____ Account #_____ Contact Person: _____ Telephone#: _____				
Name: _____ Address:_____ City: _____ State:_____ Zip: _____ Account #_____ Contact Person: _____ Telephone#: _____				
Name: _____ Address:_____ City: _____ State:_____ Zip: _____ Account #_____ Contact Person: _____ Telephone#: _____				
Name: _____ Address:_____ City: _____ State:_____ Zip: _____ Account #_____ Contact Person: _____ Telephone#: _____				
Name: _____ Address:_____ City: _____ State:_____ Zip: _____ Account #_____ Contact Person: _____ Telephone#: _____				

Summary of Debts as of _____

To Whom Owed	Balance Due	# of Payments Remaining	Interest Rate	Minimum Required Payment
Name: _____ Address:_____ City: _____ State:_____ Zip: _____ Account #_____ Contact Person: _____ Telephone#: _____				
Name: _____ Address:_____ City: _____ State:_____ Zip: _____ Account #_____ Contact Person: _____ Telephone#: _____				
Name: _____ Address:_____ City: _____ State:_____ Zip: _____ Account #_____ Contact Person: _____ Telephone#: _____				
Name: _____ Address:_____ City: _____ State:_____ Zip: _____ Account #_____ Contact Person: _____ Telephone#: _____				
Name: _____ Address:_____ City: _____ State:_____ Zip: _____ Account #_____ Contact Person: _____ Telephone#: _____				

"To the Greater Glory of God ~ Ad Majorem Dei Gloriam"

Summary of Debts as of _____

To Whom Owed	Balance Due	# of Payments Remaining	Interest Rate	Minimum Required Payment
Name: _____ Address:_____ City: _____ State:_____ Zip: _____ Account #_____ Contact Person: _____ Telephone#: _____				
Name: _____ Address:_____ City: _____ State:_____ Zip: _____ Account #_____ Contact Person: _____ Telephone#: _____				
Name: _____ Address:_____ City: _____ State:_____ Zip: _____ Account #_____ Contact Person: _____ Telephone#: _____				
Name: _____ Address:_____ City: _____ State:_____ Zip: _____ Account #_____ Contact Person: _____ Telephone#: _____				
Name: _____ Address:_____ City: _____ State:_____ Zip: _____ Account #_____ Contact Person: _____ Telephone#: _____				

"To the Greater Glory of God ~ Ad Majorem Dei Gloriam"

Summary of Debts as of _____

To Whom Owed	Balance Due	# of Payments Remaining	Interest Rate	Minimum Required Payment
Name: _____ Address:_____ City: _____ State:_____ Zip: _____ Account # _____ Contact Person: _____ Telephone#: _____				
Name: _____ Address:_____ City: _____ State:_____ Zip: _____ Account # _____ Contact Person: _____ Telephone#: _____				
Name: _____ Address:_____ City: _____ State:_____ Zip: _____ Account # _____ Contact Person: _____ Telephone#: _____				
Name: _____ Address:_____ City: _____ State:_____ Zip: _____ Account # _____ Contact Person: _____ Telephone#: _____				
Name: _____ Address:_____ City: _____ State:_____ Zip: _____ Account # _____ Contact Person: _____ Telephone#: _____				

"To the Greater Glory of God ~ Ad Majorem Dei Gloriam"

Budget Worksheet as of _____

Account Description	To Date Actual $	To Date Actual %	Annual Budget $	Annual Budget %
Gross Income				
Salary				
Bonus				
Interest				
Dividends				
Retirement Plan				
Other Investment Income				
Other				
Tithing/Almsgiving				
Deductible				
Non-deductible				
Faith Education				
Taxes				
Federal Income				
State Income				
Social Security				
Medicare				
State Disability				
Other				
Current Education				
Tuition				
Materials				
Transportation				
Other				
Savings				
Contingency				
Future Education				
Retirement				
Housing				
Mortgage/Rent				
Insurance				
Taxes				
Electricity				
Gas				
Water				
Gardening				
Housecleaning				
Telephone				
Maintenance				
Pest Control				
Association Dues				
Bottled Water				
Improvements				
Other				
Groceries				

Budget Worksheet as of _____

Account Description	To Date Actual $	To Date Actual %	Annual Budget $	Annual Budget %
Automobile				
Payments				
Gas/Oil				
Insurance				
License/Taxes				
Maintenance/Repair				
Other				
Medical Expenses				
Doctor				
Dentist				
Prescriptions				
Other				
Insurance				
Life				
Medical				
Disability				
Other				
Debt Payments				
Credit Card				
Loans and Notes				
Other				
Clothing				
Entertain. and Recreation				
Eating Out				
Child Care				
Allowances				
Activites				
Vacation				
Cable Television/Movies				
Other				
Work Related				
Education/Dues				
Clothing				
Child Care				
Other				
Miscellaneous				
Beauty/Barber/Cosmetics				
Laundry				
Subscriptions				
Holidays				
Home Expenses				
Veterinarian				
Other				
Summary of Inc./Exp.				
Total Income				
Total Expenses				
Income Over/(Under) Exp.				

Budget Worksheet as of _____

Account Description	To Date Actual $	To Date Actual %	Annual Budget $	Annual Budget %
Gross Income				
Salary				
Bonus				
Interest				
Dividends				
Retirement Plan				
Other Investment Income				
Other				
Tithing/Almsgiving				
Deductible				
Non-deductible				
Faith Education				
Taxes				
Federal Income				
State Income				
Social Security				
Medicare				
State Disability				
Other				
Current Education				
Tuition				
Materials				
Transportation				
Other				
Savings				
Contingency				
Future Education				
Retirement				
Housing				
Mortgage/Rent				
Insurance				
Taxes				
Electricity				
Gas				
Water				
Gardening				
Housecleaning				
Telephone				
Maintenance				
Pest Control				
Association Dues				
Bottled Water				
Improvements				
Other				
Groceries				

Budget Worksheet as of _____

Account Description	To Date Actual $	To Date Actual %	Annual Budget $	Annual Budget %
Automobile				
Payments				
Gas/Oil				
Insurance				
License/Taxes				
Maintenance/Repair				
Other				
Medical Expenses				
Doctor				
Dentist				
Prescriptions				
Other				
Insurance				
Life				
Medical				
Disability				
Other				
Debt Payments				
Credit Card				
Loans and Notes				
Other				
Clothing				
Entertain. and Recreation				
Eating Out				
Child Care				
Allowances				
Activites				
Vacation				
Cable Television/Movies				
Other				
Work Related				
Education/Dues				
Clothing				
Child Care				
Other				
Miscellaneous				
Beauty/Barber/Cosmetics				
Laundry				
Subscriptions				
Holidays				
Home Expenses				
Veterinarian				
Other				
Summary of Inc./Exp.				
Total Income				
Total Expenses				
Income Over/(Under) Exp.				

FINANCIAL FOUNDATIONS FOR THE FAMILY

"To the Greater Glory of God ~ Ad Majorem Dei Gloriam"

Budget Worksheet as of _____

Account Description	To Date Actual $	To Date Actual %	Annual Budget $	Annual Budget %
Gross Income				
Salary				
Bonus				
Interest				
Dividends				
Retirement Plan				
Other Investment Income				
Other				
Tithing/Almsgiving				
Deductible				
Non-deductible				
Faith Education				
Taxes				
Federal Income				
State Income				
Social Security				
Medicare				
State Disability				
Other				
Current Education				
Tuition				
Materials				
Transportation				
Other				
Savings				
Contingency				
Future Education				
Retirement				
Housing				
Mortgage/Rent				
Insurance				
Taxes				
Electricity				
Gas				
Water				
Gardening				
Housecleaning				
Telephone				
Maintenance				
Pest Control				
Association Dues				
Bottled Water				
Improvements				
Other				
Groceries				

Budget Worksheet as of _____

Account Description	To Date Actual $	To Date Actual %	Annual Budget $	Annual Budget %
Automobile				
Payments				
Gas/Oil				
Insurance				
License/Taxes				
Maintenance/Repair				
Other				
Medical Expenses				
Doctor				
Dentist				
Prescriptions				
Other				
Insurance				
Life				
Medical				
Disability				
Other				
Debt Payments				
Credit Card				
Loans and Notes				
Other				
Clothing				
Entertain. and Recreation				
Eating Out				
Child Care				
Allowances				
Activites				
Vacation				
Cable Television/Movies				
Other				
Work Related				
Education/Dues				
Clothing				
Child Care				
Other				
Miscellaneous				
Beauty/Barber/Cosmetics				
Laundry				
Subscriptions				
Holidays				
Home Expenses				
Veterinarian				
Other				
Summary of Inc./Exp.				
Total Income				
Total Expenses				
Income Over/(Under) Exp.				

FINANCIAL FOUNDATIONS FOR THE FAMILY

Budget Worksheet as of _____

Account Description	To Date Actual $	To Date Actual %	Annual Budget $	Annual Budget %
Gross Income				
Salary				
Bonus				
Interest				
Dividends				
Retirement Plan				
Other Investment Income				
Other				
Tithing/Almsgiving				
Deductible				
Non-deductible				
Faith Education				
Taxes				
Federal Income				
State Income				
Social Security				
Medicare				
State Disability				
Other				
Current Education				
Tuition				
Materials				
Transportation				
Other				
Savings				
Contingency				
Future Education				
Retirement				
Housing				
Mortgage/Rent				
Insurance				
Taxes				
Electricity				
Gas				
Water				
Gardening				
Housecleaning				
Telephone				
Maintenance				
Pest Control				
Association Dues				
Bottled Water				
Improvements				
Other				
Groceries				

Budget Worksheet as of _____

Account Description	To Date Actual $	To Date Actual %	Annual Budget $	Annual Budget %
Automobile				
Payments				
Gas/Oil				
Insurance				
License/Taxes				
Maintenance/Repair				
Other				
Medical Expenses				
Doctor				
Dentist				
Prescriptions				
Other				
Insurance				
Life				
Medical				
Disability				
Other				
Debt Payments				
Credit Card				
Loans and Notes				
Other				
Clothing				
Entertain. and Recreation				
Eating Out				
Child Care				
Allowances				
Activites				
Vacation				
Cable Television/Movies				
Other				
Work Related				
Education/Dues				
Clothing				
Child Care				
Other				
Miscellaneous				
Beauty/Barber/Cosmetics				
Laundry				
Subscriptions				
Holidays				
Home Expenses				
Veterinarian				
Other				
Summary of Inc./Exp.				
Total Income				
Total Expenses				
Income Over/(Under) Exp.				

"To the Greater Glory of God ~ Ad Majorem Dei Gloriam"

Budget Worksheet as of _____

Account Description	To Date Actual $	To Date Actual %	Annual Budget $	Annual Budget %
Gross Income				
Salary				
Bonus				
Interest				
Dividends				
Retirement Plan				
Other Investment Income				
Other				
Tithing/Almsgiving				
Deductible				
Non-deductible				
Faith Education				
Taxes				
Federal Income				
State Income				
Social Security				
Medicare				
State Disability				
Other				
Current Education				
Tuition				
Materials				
Transportation				
Other				
Savings				
Contingency				
Future Education				
Retirement				
Housing				
Mortgage/Rent				
Insurance				
Taxes				
Electricity				
Gas				
Water				
Gardening				
Housecleaning				
Telephone				
Maintenance				
Pest Control				
Association Dues				
Bottled Water				
Improvements				
Other				
Groceries				

Budget Worksheet as of _____

Account Description	To Date Actual $	To Date Actual %	Annual Budget $	Annual Budget %
Automobile				
Payments				
Gas/Oil				
Insurance				
License/Taxes				
Maintenance/Repair				
Other				
Medical Expenses				
Doctor				
Dentist				
Prescriptions				
Other				
Insurance				
Life				
Medical				
Disability				
Other				
Debt Payments				
Credit Card				
Loans and Notes				
Other				
Clothing				
Entertain. and Recreation				
Eating Out				
Child Care				
Allowances				
Activites				
Vacation				
Cable Television/Movies				
Other				
Work Related				
Education/Dues				
Clothing				
Child Care				
Other				
Miscellaneous				
Beauty/Barber/Cosmetics				
Laundry				
Subscriptions				
Holidays				
Home Expenses				
Veterinarian				
Other				
Summary of Inc./Exp.				
Total Income				
Total Expenses				
Income Over/(Under) Exp.				

FINANCIAL FOUNDATIONS FOR THE FAMILY

Budget Worksheet as of _____

Account Description	To Date Actual $	To Date Actual %	Annual Budget $	Annual Budget %
Gross Income				
Salary				
Bonus				
Interest				
Dividends				
Retirement Plan				
Other Investment Income				
Other				
Tithing/Almsgiving				
Deductible				
Non-deductible				
Faith Education				
Taxes				
Federal Income				
State Income				
Social Security				
Medicare				
State Disability				
Other				
Current Education				
Tuition				
Materials				
Transportation				
Other				
Savings				
Contingency				
Future Education				
Retirement				
Housing				
Mortgage/Rent				
Insurance				
Taxes				
Electricity				
Gas				
Water				
Gardening				
Housecleaning				
Telephone				
Maintenance				
Pest Control				
Association Dues				
Bottled Water				
Improvements				
Other				
Groceries				

Budget Worksheet as of _____

Account Description	To Date Actual $	To Date Actual %	Annual Budget $	Annual Budget %
Automobile				
Payments				
Gas/Oil				
Insurance				
License/Taxes				
Maintenance/Repair				
Other				
Medical Expenses				
Doctor				
Dentist				
Prescriptions				
Other				
Insurance				
Life				
Medical				
Disability				
Other				
Debt Payments				
Credit Card				
Loans and Notes				
Other				
Clothing				
Entertain. and Recreation				
Eating Out				
Child Care				
Allowances				
Activites				
Vacation				
Cable Television/Movies				
Other				
Work Related				
Education/Dues				
Clothing				
Child Care				
Other				
Miscellaneous				
Beauty/Barber/Cosmetics				
Laundry				
Subscriptions				
Holidays				
Home Expenses				
Veterinarian				
Other				
Summary of Inc./Exp.				
Total Income				
Total Expenses				
Income Over/(Under) Exp.				

"To the Greater Glory of God ~ Ad Majorem Dei Gloriam"

Budget Worksheet as of _____

Account Description	To Date Actual $	To Date Actual %	Annual Budget $	Annual Budget %
Gross Income				
Salary				
Bonus				
Interest				
Dividends				
Retirement Plan				
Other Investment Income				
Other				
Tithing/Almsgiving				
Deductible				
Non-deductible				
Faith Education				
Taxes				
Federal Income				
State Income				
Social Security				
Medicare				
State Disability				
Other				
Current Education				
Tuition				
Materials				
Transportation				
Other				
Savings				
Contingency				
Future Education				
Retirement				
Housing				
Mortgage/Rent				
Insurance				
Taxes				
Electricity				
Gas				
Water				
Gardening				
Housecleaning				
Telephone				
Maintenance				
Pest Control				
Association Dues				
Bottled Water				
Improvements				
Other				
Groceries				

Budget Worksheet as of _____

Account Description	To Date Actual $	To Date Actual %	Annual Budget $	Annual Budget %
Automobile	_____	_____	_____	_____
Payments	_____		_____	
Gas/Oil	_____		_____	
Insurance	_____		_____	
License/Taxes	_____		_____	
Maintenance/Repair	_____		_____	
Other	_____		_____	
Medical Expenses	_____	_____	_____	_____
Doctor	_____		_____	
Dentist	_____		_____	
Prescriptions	_____		_____	
Other	_____		_____	
Insurance	_____	_____	_____	_____
Life	_____		_____	
Medical	_____		_____	
Disability	_____		_____	
Other	_____		_____	
Debt Payments	_____	_____	_____	_____
Credit Card	_____		_____	
Loans and Notes	_____		_____	
Other	_____		_____	
Clothing	_____	_____	_____	_____
Entertain. and Recreation	_____	_____	_____	_____
Eating Out	_____		_____	
Child Care	_____		_____	
Allowances	_____		_____	
Activites	_____		_____	
Vacation	_____		_____	
Cable Television/Movies	_____		_____	
Other	_____		_____	
Work Related	_____	_____	_____	_____
Education/Dues	_____		_____	
Clothing	_____		_____	
Child Care	_____		_____	
Other	_____		_____	
Miscellaneous	_____	_____	_____	_____
Beauty/Barber/Cosmetics	_____		_____	
Laundry	_____		_____	
Subscriptions	_____		_____	
Holidays	_____		_____	
Home Expenses	_____		_____	
Veterinarian	_____		_____	
Other	_____		_____	
Summary of Inc./Exp.				
Total Income	_____	_____	_____	_____
Total Expenses	_____	_____	_____	_____
Income Over/(Under) Exp.	_____	_____	_____	_____

FINANCIAL FOUNDATIONS FOR THE FAMILY

Individual Account Register

Account Description: _____   Annual Budget:_____

Date	Check #	Description	Amount	Cumulative Total

"To the Greater Glory of God ~ Ad Majorem Dei Gloriam"

Individual Account Register

Account Description: _____   Annual Budget:_____

Date	Check #	Description	Amount	Cumulative Total

"To the Greater Glory of God ~ Ad Majorem Dei Gloriam"

Individual Account Register

Account Description: _____   Annual Budget:_____

Date	Check #	Description	Amount	Cumulative Total

"To the Greater Glory of God ~ Ad Majorem Dei Gloriam"

Individual Account Register

Account Description: _____   Annual Budget:_____

Date	Check #	Description	Amount	Cumulative Total

Individual Account Register

Account Description: _____   Annual Budget:_____

Date	Check #	Description	Amount	Cumulative Total

"To the Greater Glory of God ~ Ad Majorem Dei Gloriam"

Individual Account Register

Account Description: _____   Annual Budget:_____

Date	Check #	Description	Amount	Cumulative Total

FINANCIAL FOUNDATIONS FOR THE FAMILY

"To the Greater Glory of God ~ Ad Majorem Dei Gloriam"

Individual Account Register

Account Description: _____   Annual Budget:_____

Date	Check #	Description	Amount	Cumulative Total

Use the order form below to order additional copies of Finances for Today's Catholic Family or other resources from Financial Foundations for the Family.

Order Form

Code	Title	Quantity	Unit Price	Total Price
B0002	Finances for Today's Catholic Family		12.95	
B0003	The Family Financial Organizer		14.95	
B0001	Your Family Finances – Worry & Anxiety or Peace & Contentment Brochure (Minimum Order 25)		.20/ea.	

Tax on Subtotal (CA Residents only, 7.25%) $_____

Shipping Charge $_____
(See chart below)

Charitable Contributions*$_____

Total Enclosed $_____

Name_____ Telephone _____

Address _____

City/State/Zip _____

Return order and payment to:
Financial Foundations for the Family
P.O. Box 890998, Temecula, CA 92589-0998
Phone 909-699-7066
Fax 909-308-4539

Shipping Charges

Amount of Order	Priority Mail/UPS	2nd Day Delivery
Up to $10.00	2.95	11.95
$10.01 - $25.00	4.95	12.95
$25.01 - $40.00	5.95	13.95
$40.01 - $50.00	6.95	14.95
$50.01 - $75.00	7.95	15.95
$75.01 - 100.00	8.95	17.95
Over $100.00	9%	19.95

Financial Foundtions for the Family is a 501(c)(3) non-profit organization recognized for tax-deductible giving by the federal government.